Women's Devotional Talks
for special occasions

by CAROL K. WOLF

illustrated by Olga Packard

STANDARD PUBLISHING
Cincinnati, Ohio   2976

Dedicated to my daughters,
Peggy and Beth,
with whom I've learned so much
about being a family.

Library of Congress Catalog Card Number: 84-50264

ISBN 0-87239-745-9

©1984 by The STANDARD PUBLISHING Company, Cincinnati, Ohio
Division of STANDEX INTERNATIONAL Corporation.
Printed in U.S.A.

Contents

FROM THE AUTHOR: These messages can be used as they are printed, or they can be used as a model around which to build your own message.

Personalize the messages as much as possible. Use the honoree's name and add events that you may know about her that will fit with the theme.

The Bible verses are all from the King James Version of the Bible. You may prefer using a more modern translation. The verses can be changed to others you may choose.

The decoration suggestions are just ideas and not necessary to the success of the message. The gifts are not totally necessary either, although they help the honoree or women to recall the message as the gifts are used.

All messages should be closed with prayer.

Learning From Bread

Scripture: "Jesus said unto them, I am the bread of life: he that cometh to me shall never hunger; and he that believeth on me shall never thirst" (John 6:35).

Gifts: Small plaques for each person, made as follows—Cut small pieces of wood (something with one side finished, such as paneling), about 4" wide by 5" high. Bake tiny loaves of bread. When these are cool, cover them with two coats of clear shellac and let them dry. Glue a spike of wheat and a few colorful strawflowers to a plaque, then glue on the loaf of bread. Add a ribbon bow. A larger plaque can be made for the bride. Add a verse of Scripture to hers, such as John 6:35.

Decorations: Bake large loaves of bread for the table centerpieces. When they are cool, cover them with two coats of clear shellac and let them dry. Use colorful ribbon, about ½" wide, to tie around the bread. Add several spikes of wheat and some strawflowers as you tie the ribbon in a bow. These can be used as prizes for the games and/or door prizes.

Devotion:
It is difficult to live without bread. If you've ever run out of bread you know what I mean. You need bread for toast in the morning. You need bread for sandwiches, whether you pack a lunch or eat at home. You

need bread to make dressing, to make bread pudding, and for croutons. Bread even helps to fill up holes in growing kids!

If you haven't already done so, learn to bake bread. When things get rough, or when you feel blue, or for no particular reason at all, bake bread.

Take a large bowl to mix the dough. Assemble the ingredients. Look at the yeast. It isn't pretty, and it doesn't smell particularly good. Yet there is tremendous power in that little package!

The yeast disappears quickly as you mix it with the flour, water, salt, and shortening, but it is still there . When the dough is mixed, turn it out and knead it. The yeast has become useful, even beautiful! Because of the yeast, the dough will grow. It will be a living thing. But as it grows, it sometimes becomes unruly. Have you ever seen yeast dough that has been left too long? It grows and spills over the sides of the bowl. You have to knock it down! Then you mold it into rolls and bread loaves that puff up to be all satiny and smooth.

Now bake the bread. Have you ever walked into a kitchen where someone is baking bread? The smell! Folks respond in a special way when they smell bread baking. And you are already sharing your bread with them through the aroma.

Finally your product is finished. It is a thing of beauty, made with your own hands, a small part of you. It is ready to be enjoyed, savored, and nourishing to those who eat it.

Married life is much like a loaf of bread. Day by day you will become more beautiful and useful, just as the yeast does. You'll be more serious. You'll have a definite purpose in your life—to please your husband. Soon you will be knit together in a common goal—to have a happy home.

Frustrations will come. The car won't start, the washer won't go. The milk gets spilled and the plant gets knocked over. And all this in the same day! Remember the bread? How it has to be kneaded to get it into the right shape? You will require some kneading to get you in shape, especially when frustrations come. There is a place to go for calming down. God will help. Let Him knead you and mold you.

There may be times when you grow unruly. Like the unruly dough, you will need to be knocked down! Hebrews 12:6 tells us, "For whom the Lord loveth he chasteneth." Read God's Word; listen to Him. Pray for His guidance and help. Then be ready to do what He expects of you. And don't sit back and dry out. Bread isn't very good when it dries out, and we often throw it away. You won't be very useful if you dry out. Listen to what the apostle Paul says about this: "I keep under my body, and bring it into subjection: lest that by any means, when I have preached to others, I myself should be a castaway" (1 Corinthians 9:27). Be careful that your life is right or you'll be cast away as dry bread is cast out.

After you become proficient at bread baking, you will find great joy in giving bread as a gift. Give at least one loaf from each batch. So few women bake bread and so many people love homemade bread! Share it with a sick friend, a neighbor, or a busy mother. Jesus, in Mark 9:41, says, "Whosoever shall give you a cup of water to drink in my name, because ye belong to Christ, verily I say unto you, he shall not lose his reward." Water or bread, when needed, is a great blessing!

Be sure your home honors Christ in all things. Have prayer before meals; language that is always sweet; a lot of love; and above all, God in first place.

Share your home with friends and family, and even with strangers. Others enjoy a Christian home. There seem to be so few Christian homes nowadays. It is an honor for you to have one.

When your children come, mold them, love them, and discipline them. Then you'll see them grow to be useful and beautiful too, a blessing to others, just like that loaf of homemade bread!

Clothesline Flutterings

Scripture: "Thy wife shall be a fruitful vine by the sides of thine house" (Psalm 128:3).

Gift: A sturdy plastic clothes basket can be filled with a clothesline, clothespins, laundry detergent, fabric softener, and other laundry needs.

Decorations: Purchase child-size clothes baskets and fill them with flowers, real or silk. You will need a container in the bottom to hold the flowers, and water for the real ones.

Devotion:
Most of you probably have automatic washers and dryers in your homes. They are great. They save both work and time. This is important in our busy lives. But, do you ever get the urge to hang your clothes outside to dry? Think about this with me.

1. Just about everyone of you has, at one time or another, had a weight problem. And how are you told to lose this weight? Well, it's exercise—up and down, up and down. Hanging clothes on the line can give you that up-and-down exercise in no time! And if your washers are in the basement, climbing the steps helps too!

And each article of clothing you bend down for should remind you of the person who wore it. Give thanks for that person. Remember where he or she wore the garment and be glad for the happy times.

2. Isn't it fun to see a line of clothes blowing in the wind, sometimes slowly, sometimes as fast as possible, and sometimes so hard they will barely stay on the line!

Hanging clothes outside in winter is another adventure! Before you finish hanging the clothes, they are frozen stiff! Have you ever tried to bring a pair of frozen long underwear or overalls into the house? They will hardly fit through the door!

3. You certainly take note of the weather more when you hang your wash outside. How you appreciate a pretty day! All too many people work in windowless rooms and never know what kind of a day the Lord has given.

4. When you hang your clothes outside you are more aware of your neighbors. You note their comings and goings, who has a new baby, who is sick, or who has troubles. And getting to know your neighbors is the first step in winning them to the Lord!

5. Drying clothes in an automatic dryer just doesn't give them that beautiful, fresh-air smell that the outdoors gives. Isn't it a great feeling to crawl into bed between freshly laundered sheets that have been dried outdoors!

6. Occasionally there are times when you need help urgently as you hang your wash. The clothesline snaps! And you are left holding up the wet clothes so they won't become soiled. All you can do is call for help—anyone will do. Then you must start hanging the clothes all over again when the line is repaired.

7. When you have too many heavy pieces of clothing on a line, what happens? Yes, the line begins to sag and you have to prop it up with a clothes pole. Most of today's children probably don't even know what one of these is.

8. The best part is the satisfaction you get when you have taken soiled, wrinkled clothing and linens and turned them into clean, fresh-smelling piles of laundry, ready to be used again.

Now, what does this have to do with you, our bride-to-be? You say, "I'll never hang my clothes outside." Maybe you don't even have a place to hang them. Let's make some applications.

1. Every marriage has its ups and downs. It is so easy to run home to Mom during the down times! Don't give in to this temptation. Rather, let the down times draw you closer to your husband. And when he is down, stand by, quietly, to help him. The up times are easy to take, but they don't usually last too long. Enjoy them and also try to find something in each day you can feel good about.

2. As you visualize clothes blowing in the wind, realize that life is much

like this—some days will be dull, no wind blowing. Other days will go along quickly and smoothly—a lively breeze. Then others will be stormy, windy, and rough. You'll have to work on the slow days to make them interesting. Don't let the day-by-day chores make you dull and boring. Prepare something special for dinner. Make or buy your husband a small gift, for no reason at all. These things can also help smooth the stormy days. Remember Psalm 128:3, "Thy wife shall be a fruitful vine by the sides of thine house."

3. Those frozen clothes can teach you a lesson. The stiff overalls that won't bend are a picture of you when you refuse to bend! Don't be so stubborn that you refuse to bend to your husband, or someday you may not have him to bend to! Turn off the TV or radio, put down the book or newspaper, and have a quiet time with the Lord—both of you. Renew your love for your Lord every day and your love for each other will grow. Proverbs 17:1 says, "Better is a dry morsel and quietness therewith, than a house full of sacrifices with strife."

4. Your family, your friends, and your neighbors must all be important to you. "A man that hath friends must show himself friendly" (Proverbs 18:24). Invite your friends into your home. You don't always have to GO somewhere. Take time to include your neighbors in your hospitality. Those who come into your home will be the people your children remember. They will learn a valuable lesson from this—home is where you gather with friends and loved ones, where you can talk and share and be happy.

5. Enjoy every good day to the limit. If there are small disagreements, work ever so quietly to get over the bumps and enjoy the day. Your spouse may not even realize there was a problem. Where will you find the answers? Go to God's Word, "meditate therein day and night." Then enjoy the benefits you reap.

6. There will be times you call for help. There may be times of deep trouble. You may think you can't talk to anyone, but, there is One who is ever near and ready to listen. He has promised never to leave us. "Be strong and of a good courage; be not afraid, neither be thou dismayed: for the Lord thy God is with thee whithersoever thou goest" (Joshua 1:9). He will hold you up and help you begin again.

7. There are usually family and friends who will want to prop you up when life gets heavy. "The aged women likewise, that they be in behavior as becometh holiness" (Titus 2:3). Paul indicates that the older women are to be teachers and examples to the younger women. Learn to accept advice (and perhaps criticism) from older women who have had the same problems you are facing. Profit from their experiences.

8. The finished product is a happy life. It takes a lot of work, a lot of love, a lot of understanding! You can do it! Proverbs says, "Whoso findeth a wife findeth a good thing, and obtaineth favor of the Lord" (18:22). It's worth it all!

10

Recipe for a Happy Family

1 Husband
1 Wife
Children (several)
1 Home
1 Bible for each
Generous portion of prayer
3 Cups of LOVE, packed
1 Package of WORK
1 Package of PLAY—together
1 Tablespoon of PATIENCE
1 Paddle, small
1 Cup of kisses

Mix thoroughly and sprinkle with awareness.

Bake in moderate oven of everyday life, using as fuel all the grudges and unpleasantness. Cool. Turn out onto platter of cheerfulness. Garnish with tears and laughter. And in large helpings, serve God, Country, and Community.

Reprinted with permission from *Farm Wife News,* P.O. Box 743, Milwaukee, WI 53201.

Putting the Pieces Together

Scripture: "And Ruth said, Entreat me not to leave thee, or to return from following after thee: for whither thou goest, I will go; and where thou lodgest, I will lodge: thy people shall be my people, and thy God my God" (Ruth 1:16).

Decorations: A display of quilts—some old, some new, at least one fancy appliqued one if possible.

Gifts: For the bride-to-be, a framed quilt block. For the mothers of the bride and groom, smaller framed quilt blocks. Patterns for these can be found in any quilt magazine or at most yard-goods stores.

Devotion:

The fad in craft work right now is quilting. Some of you have done quilting for years and know more about it than do those who are now teaching it.

How about a quilting lesson? You may not want to quilt, but perhaps after this you'll appreciate a quilt more the next time you see one.

Around your home you have pieces of cloth. Some you've had for years—mostly scraps from former sewing projects. Then there is usually a new piece you've saved to make just the right article.

The day comes. You take a quilting course or see a quilt you'd love to make and you get excited! So you take out your trusty scissors and start cutting. You cut so many of this shape and so many of that one. You even use that pretty piece of cloth you have been saving.

These pieces of cloth become your paints as you learn to work with colors. Some are rich and vibrant, others rather dull and uninteresting. You keep putting different ones together until you find some that complement each other. What satisfaction there is in finding just the right combination!

Next, you sew these pieces of cloth together to make a new piece of cloth. This is your quilt top, your design.

Now comes the hard part. For this you need a quilting frame or hoops. You put the back of the quilt on the frame first, then the batting or filling, and finally your new designed piece on top. These must be stretched tight and kept very straight.

You are now ready to begin the actual quilting. You haven't been quilting until now, only piecing. Good quilting is not easy. It consists of many, many tiny, even stitches that must go through all three layers on the frame. You prick your fingers many times. The frame shifts. Sometimes you find you have stitched in the wrong places. But it is fun to see the pattern being accented, and to see how lovely your new design really is.

Making a quilt takes time. Some women work years on one quilt. Quilting is used on wall hangings, pictures, pillows, even window quilts that save heat. Quilts for beds come in all sizes, from tiny baby quilts to king-size quilts. No matter what the size, all are appreciated and dearly loved.

Many quilts are mended over and over, because they are a part of the owner's life. They contain pieces of dresses, skirts, shirts, or slacks that remind the owners of happy times gone by. Quilts are made with love. That's why it's so hard to give or sell a quilt.

You remember, in the book of Ruth, how Naomi decided to return to her former home, Bethlehem in Judah. Orpah, one of her daughters-in-law, remained in her own country of Moab. But Ruth, the other daughter-in-law, decided to leave Moab and go with Naomi. Ruth 1:14 says, "They lifted up their voice, and wept again: and Orpah kissed her mother-in-law; but Ruth clave unto her."

Ruth continues, "Entreat me not to leave thee, or to return from following after thee: for whither thou goest, I will go; and where thou lodgest, I will lodge: thy people shall be my people, and thy God my God: where thou diest, will I die, and there will I be buried: the Lord do so to me, and more also, if aught but death part thee and me" (Ruth 1:16, 17).

Ruth begins to cut out a new life for herself. She cuts many little pieces. She leaves Orpah, she leaves her home country and family. She goes into a whole new situation in another country and home.

In Bethlehem, Naomi encourages Ruth to glean in the field of a man named Boaz, and, surely, while Ruth is out there, Naomi prays for her. In time, Ruth and Boaz find that they complement each other. This is the beginning of a new design, a new family.

13

Today, brides do not have to be redeemed or paid for as Ruth had to be. Boaz had to work out an arrangement for Naomi's land and for marrying Ruth. After everything was settled, Boaz says he has "purchased his wife" and in Ruth 4:13, "Boaz took Ruth, and she was his wife."

There was a new family with a praying and happy mother-in-law. Out of this new family would come a son named Obed, and from his line would come David, and finally the Lord Jesus Christ.

There are lessons for all of us from the making of a quilt as well as from the beautiful story of Ruth.

You began your life at home with Mom and Dad who knew you had possibilities. Little by little, you started to cut out a life of your own. You cut it in many shapes—first school, then college, new friends, a job *(add personal details here)*.

You begin to put the pieces together, using various colors, trying to find the right course for your life. Then that special someone comes into your life, and you know it is the right combination. You complement each other—that is, you complete each other.

This is the beginning of a new design, a new family. No one else will ever have a family such as you will have, because there will never be another two people exactly like you!

As in quilting, you have three layers. Can you see the picture of this "quilt"? Your husband-to-be's family is on the back of this "quilt." Your family is in the center, and your new family is the "quilt top" or design. Both of your families will uphold you with prayer just as Naomi prayed for Ruth. Mothers never get away from that responsibility!

Even though you have two loving families to help you, you'll need someone else to keep your marriage a strong one. Your "quilt" of life must be held together by God. He makes up the stitches that bind the whole together. Of course, there will be pricks—disappointments and sorrows—but with God there to make you strong, life will be a beautiful design to be cherished over the years.

A happy marriage takes time. Some take years to smooth off the stubborn edges. David prayed for the Lord to teach him "good judgement and knowledge" (Psalm 119:66). Have prayer together at meal times. Take time to pray before you leave for work. Pray at the close of the day. When you ask for God's help, He will surely give it.

Just as you would protect a cherished quilt, guard your marriage. Hold it together with love—for each other and for God. And learn to show that love in many ways. Give a gift when it is least expected. Put a love note in his lunchbox, or tuck one in his shirt pocket. When he leaves for work, don't give him a peck on the cheek, but rather give him a kiss he'll remember all day. Love will be the glue that holds your marriage together, the honey that keeps it sweet. Spread it on lavishly and often. Make the most of each day you have. This poem expresses the importance of loving *today*.

14

Remember the day I borrowed your brand new car
     and dented it?
I thought you'd kill me, but you didn't.
And remember the time I dragged you to the beach,
     and you said it would rain, and it did?
I thought you'd say, "I told you so." But you didn't.
Do you remember the time I flirted with all the
     guys to make you jealous, and you were?
I thought you'd leave me, but you didn't.
Do you remember the time I spilled strawberry pie
     all over your car rug?
I thought you'd hit me, but you didn't.

. . . .

Yes, there were lots of things you didn't do.
But you put up with me, and you loved me, and you
     protected me.
There were lots of things I wanted to make up to
     you when you returned from Viet Nam.
But you didn't.*

—Leo F. Buscaglia

Your "family quilt" will be appreciated more and more as the years go by. You may have to mend some places along the way, but this will only make it more precious, a part of you. Proverbs 12:4 says, "A virtuous woman is a crown to her husband." As you give of yourself, you will become your husband's crown.

May you have a blessed and happy life together.

*From *Living, Loving, and Learning,* by Leo F. Buscaglia. ©1982. Used by permission.

Aprons, Aprons

Scripture: "The name of the Lord is a strong tower: the righteous runneth into it, and is safe" (Proverbs 18:10).

Gifts: Have an apron for the bride-to-be, either a modern cover-up or a dressy hostess type. Have aprons for the mothers also. Explain to them that they can use their aprons to wipe a tear or two after praying for the newlyweds.

Decorations: Have a display of as many different kinds of aprons as possible, from old fashioned to modern. For favors, make tiny aprons for each guest. For each miniature apron, cut a piece of cloth about 4″ wide by 3½″ high. Gather the top of the piece and stitch this to a belt 6″ long and ½″ wide. The edges do not have to be finished. You may want to trim around the bottom of the apron with pinking shears. Decorate each apron with a small artificial flower.

Devotion:

There is one thing that's disappearing from the homemakers' world. That's an apron! Aprons are definitely old fashioned. Genesis 3:7 mentions aprons made of fig leaves, so you see aprons have been around a long time!

Few young people wear aprons nowadays. Maybe this is because dresses are wash and wear. It's just as easy to wash a dress as it is to wash an apron. Or perhaps it is because so many women wear slacks, jeans, or shorts. Aprons just don't go with those!

In Grandma's and Great-Grandma's days, one wouldn't be properly dressed unless one had on an apron. For everyday, a homemaker wore a long apron with big pockets. For Sundays and special days, she wore a shorter, fancier one. Dresses were long, and certainly not wash and wear! It was far easier to scrub an apron than a big dress. Everyday aprons were usually made of a small print or gingham and of dark colors. These had to be washed and ironed less often.

When callers came, one simply removed the dirty apron and reached for a clean one, or as some did, turned the used one inside out, and presto! one was ready for guests.

Grandma's apron was great to wipe away a small child's tears, to clean a scraped knee, to cover a wee child for an unexpected nap, to serve as a bib when a napkin wasn't near, or to be used as a hiding place for a shy child when strangers came around.

Grandma might have used her apron as a basket for baby chicks she found under a hen in the field. She would carry the little things into the house to get them warm. Aprons were used to bring back puppies or kittens that strayed from their boxes to explore the new world. Aprons were used to carry kindling or corncobs to start a fire in the pot-bellied stove. One apronful was just the right amount.

When Grandma went for a walk and found hickory nuts or ripe apples, up came the apron to carry them home. It was always fun, in the spring, to find the first pussywillows and flowers. Again, the apron carried them home.

Today, magazines and gadget catalogs tell us to use a tray to carry furniture polish, dust rags, and findings as you clean. Grandma used an apron with big pockets, and some women still do.

Have you ever seen anyone shoo chickens or drive pigs with an apron? Cut-offs or jeans can never fill that place! Hickory nuts and apples won't fit in or feel good in cut-offs either!

Wrapped bits of hard candy were great to have as Grandma went through her day. They were in her apron pocket, of course. And after talking to a neighbor or a friend for a while, it was ever so nice to just happen to have a recipe in that pocket to share with that neighbor or friend.

Psalm 57:1 says, "Be merciful unto me, O God, be merciful unto me: for my soul trusteth in thee: yea, in the shadow of thy wings will I make my refuge, until these calamities be overpast." The apron is a picture of our Lord's protection and caring for us in difficult times.

Many a woman has cried into her apron. (Grandma didn't have Kleenex!) It was so good to cover her face and then wipe away the tears, whether they were tears of sadness, disappointment, happiness, or joy.

You won't have to wear an apron the way women used to. You probably won't be carrying home hickory nuts or apples, or baby chickens.

An apron is a bit old fashioned. Many other old-fashioned things besides aprons have gone. But some are still new. Proverbs 31:27, 28 tells us, "She looketh well to the ways of her household, and eateth not the bread of idleness. Her children arise up, and call her blessed; her husband also, and he praiseth her." While these words were written thousands of years ago, they are as true now as they were when they were written. The woman who takes care of her house and children will receive a rich reward—not necessarily a monetary reward, but the love, honor, and blessings of her children and husband.

You are taking on a big job. You'll need help many times. Seek your help from the Lord Jesus Christ, who is ever old, yet ever new, and always ever near. "The name of the Lord is a strong tower: the righteous runneth into it, and is safe."

Take the Lord into the new family unit you are starting. Knowing He is ever near will be a great comfort to you. Let your lives and your home show others that you know and love God and His Son Jesus. Be comfortable with the Lord, so that when you need "a strong tower" you'll know just where to go!

Lessons From Housecleaning

Scripture: "She will do him good and not evil all the days of her life" (Proverbs 31:12). Have this printed on programs or on a small poster to be placed near the speaker's place.

Gifts: For the bride-to-be, a plaque with the words "Am I Fun to Live With?" This can be done in decoupage, counted cross-stitch, or embroidery.

Decorations: For each table (or for head table only), flower arrangements in child-size sand buckets. Have a miniature broom and/or mop sticking in each arrangement.

Devotion:
Your house (or apartment) is probably painted, cleaned, and polished. Everything is in place, cabinets neatly arranged, ready for you to move in. Along about next spring, however, you'll take a good look at your home and find it needs housecleaning!

Whatever happened to that old institution—spring housecleaning? Many people never spring clean any more. With super vacuum cleaners, no-wax floors, quick-dry paint, and prepasted wallpaper, one can do all this work after having worked away from home all day!

There still are, however, a few who do houseclean. Some do it one room at a time, while others turn the whole house upside down. That's what makes it fun and makes the worker stick to it!

Whether you tear up everything at once, or work systematically, one room at a time, you still do the same things. As you move the furniture around and go through the drawers and cupboards, you find such interesting things. It may be an old locket, or a newspaper clipping, a new pattern you've never used, or that blouse you didn't get around to mending. You sit a bit and think about each thing, then put it on the I'll-take-care-of-that-later pile. Granted, next spring you'll find it again, but for one year it will be out of sight!

Once you start, you find so much that needs to be done—clothes to be mended, buttons to be sewed on, drawers that need fixing, walls that could stand a coat of paint. And you always wonder how anyone found anything in that closet!

The mattress must be turned, and you decide to rearrange the furniture, but you can't budge the dresser. Then you enlist the not-too-willing aid of your husband, who has probably been saying such things as, "When will this be over? . . . Where did you put my magazines? . . . What happened to my favorite sneakers? . . . Where can I sit tonight?" But finally he can say, "I'm glad that's over for another year!"

There are lessons to be learned even from cleaning house. Once in awhile you need to turn off the TV or put down that book, and after dishes are done, sit down and think. "How well are we doing? What areas need a bit more kindness? Do I need to polish up my manners and attitudes? Or rearrange my priorities? Do my meals need perking up? Am I fun to live with, or have I become a grouch, someone who complains or nags, or even uses sharp words?"

There may be days when you'll have to turn your life upside down and clean out a lot of things you thought were great. Your time may need to be spent differently from what you thought it would be. You may want something badly but know you can't have it. Maybe the two of you can't agree on something that really isn't very important. All of these problems must be looked at, studied, and perhaps rearranged or even thrown out. The apostle Paul says in Philippians 4:11, "I have learned, in whatsoever state I am, therewith to be content." Some days you'll need to read that verse over and over again.

Your job as a wife is to make your husband happy. (And of course, his job is to make you happy.) You'll soon learn how to accomplish that. Remember to greet each other with a smile, a hug and kiss, rather than with all the day's problems and disappointments. Proverbs 31:12 says of the virtuous woman, "She will do him good and not evil all the days of her life." You see, these are your orders.

Both your mother and your mother-in-law will be ready to help you.

They may even be tempted to give too much advice! They'll want to tell you how to do something, especially if they've experienced the problem. It's so hard for mothers to see their children stumble and fall. But you must fall and learn to pick yourselves up again. This helps you to grow and draws you closer together. The scars help to make a stronger relationship. Mothers, just watch, keep still, and pray. Remember the words from Ecclesiastes: "One generation passeth away, and another generation cometh." This new generation will do all right if you let them work out their own problems.

Most women, as they houseclean, like to put something new in the house. It may be just a small decoration, some new curtains, or a piece of furniture, new or refinished. Every day can hold something new in it for your marriage. Here's how: Keep a devotion book and your Bible handy. Set aside a certain time each day and let nothing keep you from your time with God. Lamentations 3:22 and 23 tell us, "It is of the Lord's mercies that we are not consumed, because his compassions fail not. They are new every morning: great is thy faithfulness." His blessings will be new every day if you will only accept them. Seek that exciting bit every day for your marriage. And remember to ask yourself each day, "Am I fun to live with?" If the answer is "No!" sit still, think, pray, ask, and then act!

A Full Cup

Scripture: "My cup runneth over" (Psalm 23:5).

Gift: A pretty cup and saucer can be given to the bride at the end of the message.

Decorations: Have arrangements of small real or silk flowers in decorative cups and saucers on each table, or arrange several of these on a serving table.

Devotion:

Philippians 4 should be required study before every wedding. While it doesn't mention marriage, its principles do fit. Listen while I read Philippians 4:4-13, 19, 20.

(Go back and read verse 4 aloud.) The word *rejoice* means to make glad, to fill with joy. And we're told to rejoice always. We need to keep on rejoicing every day.

(Read verse 5.) Don't be afraid or ashamed to let others know you are a Christian. Let them see by your lives that you know God and belong to Him!

(Read verse 6.) This is a recipe for peace in your daily walk. Be careful for nothing—do not worry. Be thankful for anything and everything.

(Read verse 7.) This verse should help to keep you from worrying. Sometimes you get the "worry germ" and it can tie you in knots. You won't feel this way if you have God's peace in your heart.

(Read verse 8.) This is a recipe for thinking and living. When your hearts and minds are filled with these important things, your lives will show it.

(Read verse 9.) Mark 9:41 says that if you give a cup of water in Christ's name, you shall not lose your reward. Perhaps a neighbor will come to your door to borrow a cup of sugar. This may be your opportunity to speak for Jesus. Be careful to do your best.

(Read verse 10.) Paul rejoices over the care the Philippians gave him. They must have had close fellowship with Paul before this. They knew of his needs. Close fellowship with Christian friends is essential to a happy life in Christ.

Put this verse in modern-day thinking. The Philippians probably had Paul in for a cup of coffee, a meal, or a time of rest, whenever he passed that way. They sat around the table and talked. Paul could kick off his sandals and relax. He was free to discuss his concerns and cares.

Today, when someone is asked into our homes for coffee, tea, or a glass of lemonade, it is also a time to enjoy each other, to share joys as well as problems. Take time to share your home with others. You will all be blessed.

You won't need to prepare a banquet in order to make others happy. Remember the Shunamite woman in 2 Kings 4? Elisha, the man of God, could stop by her home for food as he passed by. Maybe there was just something simple—a peanut butter and jelly sandwich, but he was welcome. This led to a desire to offer greater hospitality to Elisha. The woman's husband built a special room for Elisha so that he might stay overnight.

Lydia, the seller of purple, took Paul and his helpers in after she became a Christian. Hospitality seems to go with the Christian life. It's part of God's plan for us.

(Read verse 11.) What a verse! Some days it's hard to be content, isn't it! You will not have everything you want, but there is a joy in being content with what you have. There may be hard times, sorrow, heartbreak, and disappointments. Like you do with a handleless cup, you'll have to turn these times around. Cry for a while, then pick up the pieces, discard the unusable ones, and go on doing the best you can with what is left. Proverbs 15:16 tells us, "Better is little with the fear of the Lord, than great treasure and trouble therewith."

During the depression days, one lady had a teacup without a handle in her cupboard. When she had a few pennies left over, she would put them in the teacup. Then, when her husband wanted to take their children to town, she would reach into the teacup and get her few pennies. What joy her children received from those few pennies she had saved in the "useless" cup! The woman turned a broken cup into a happy time.

In Genesis 8, Joseph put a cup into Benjamin's bag of grain. There had been hard, unhappy times for Benjamin's family before this. That cup led to a family reunion and prosperity!

Sometimes, when a loved one dies, the family gets together. Often they have not seen each other for years. In spite of the grief of death, there is sweet fellowship. Sadness is turned into a happy, blessed time. Learn to turn the broken cups into blessed times. Let the Lord lead. It's great to see how He works. His strength is sufficient.

(Read verse 13.) What a positive statement this is. And what courage it can give you! Never be guilty of stopping too soon as you read this. "I can do all things" is only the beginning, not a complete thought. "Through Christ which strengtheneth me" is the key. The reverse is just as true—Without Christ I can do nothing. How humbling!

(Read verse 19.) God gives you more than enough. He fills your cup to overflowing. Luke 6:38 says, "Give, and it shall be given unto you; good measure, pressed down, and shaken together, and running over, shall men give into your bosom." (This has been called the "brown sugar" verse.) And make sure you are carrying a saucer under your cup when God is filling it! When you give as this verse says, you can expect blessings untold. He promises His blessings shall overtake you.

Psalm 23 says the same thing: "My cup runneth over." We can't imagine the volume of His riches, but He will more than fill your cup. He will overflow it! Don't be like the folks who complain when their coffee cup runs over, but rather rejoice and praise the Lord when yours overflows!

After you are married, make sure that you read Philippians at least once a month, and "rejoice in the Lord always: and again I say, Rejoice"!

A Little Pillow Talk

Scripture: "Keep me as the apple of the eye; hide me under the shadow of thy wings" (Psalm 17:8).

Gifts: Have an accent pillow, perhaps embroidered or with candlewicking, for the bride. For the mothers of the bride and groom, make fancy pillow-shaped pincushions. To make these, cut two pieces of pretty material for each, 5" by 6". Place a piece of gathered lace around the edge of one piece and stitch in place (see sketch). Put right sides of pillow together, with lace inside, and stitch around the pillow, leaving about 2" open for turning the pillow. Turn pillow right side out, then stuff with clean wood shavings and close with a whipping stitch.

Decorations: Make smaller pincushions to place at each person's plate at refreshment time. Use material cut in 3½" squares for these and make the same way you did the larger pincushions.

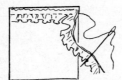

Devotion:
We're going to be talking about some household items that are quite old, yet still new. You use these every day of your lives. Most homes have many of these, in many shapes and sizes, and used in a variety of ways. As

you have probably guessed by now, I'm talking about pillows. Let's see what we can learn about these common household items.

Listen to this and think how long we've been using pillows. The Bible tells us in Genesis 28 about the trip Jacob took to Padan-Aram to find himself a wife. There were no motels along the way. When Jacob became tired, he found some stones and "put them for his pillows, and lay down in that place to sleep."

In 1 Samuel 19, Michal, David's wife, helped her husband flee from King Saul. After David had made his escape over the wall, Michal made an image like David to put in his bed and used a pillow of goat's hair, covering all this with a cloth.

Mark 4 tells of a storm at sea. Jesus was on a ship, crossing the sea. The crew became very frightened and called for Jesus. They found Him asleep on a pillow in the hinder part of the ship.

Pillows have been around a long time!

Let's think a little about the many kinds of pillows and the many uses we make of them.

1. There are "sit on" pillows or harem pillows. These can be simply old chair cushions, or they can be fancy ones with tassels on them. These are handy to have when lots of folks are around. Two people can share one of these large pillows. Girls like these pillows when their friends come over. They can sit back to back, lie on their tummies, or lean on their elbows as they talk, study, or watch TV.

2. There are large, soft pillows used on sofas or big chairs to make us more comfortable. These, too, are often used by two friends who want to sit close but need something soft to cover the hard bones!

3. Most homes have several "old" pillows. These can be taken outside when you want to lie under a tree and enjoy the clouds that roll by, to listen to the birds, or just to think.

4. Then there are the large bed pillows we are all acquainted with. These are comfortable pillows that help us have a good night's rest.

5. Sometimes we use our arms for pillows when we don't have anything better. We just put our heads down on our arms for a little snooze at the desk or table.

6. Sometimes you have NO pillow at all. But you *can* rest without a pillow if you have to.

7. Then there are accent pillows you place on your bed or sofa, or chair. These are sometimes called "throw" pillows. These are fun pillows that make your room look nice.

8. Some pillows are filled with feathers. Many people feel that feather pillows are the "real" ones. Those filled with foam, or some type of polyester, are just "artificial." Remember what was used in Michal's time—goats' hair.

Now, you're probably asking, "What does this have to do with a bridal shower?"

1. As you go into the grandest event that will ever happen to you, it would be good for you to have a large "sit on" pillow. This pillow can remind you that married life is, indeed, a time of sharing, a time of growing, a time of giving—not 50-50, but 100 percent. Maybe you'll have to give the whole pillow, without even a space for your elbows. It's worth it. A man needs to be given lots of love. He loves being loved! And giving is fun! Ephesians 5:22, 23 tells us, "Wives, submit yourselves unto your own husbands, as unto the Lord. For the husband is the head of the wife, even as Christ is the head of the church." And, of course, husbands are admonished to "love your wives, even as Christ also loved the church" (v. 25).

2. The cushion pillows—the ones that cover the bones—will be used throughout your lives together. In Psalm 17:8 there is a "cushion pillow": "Keep me as the apple of the eye; hide me under the shadow of thy wings." Work together to get over the rough spots that come along. Talk to each other! When children come, do praise the Lord for them and work together to rear them for the Lord. Be thankful that He has promised to keep you under His wings.

3. The "old" pillows are so important! Psalm 24:1 is an "old pillow": "The earth is the Lord's and the fulness therein." Think of all the Lord has given you! You and your husband will both need time to think, to clear your heads. You'll need time alone—to read, to enjoy a record, to listen to a sermon, to work out a puzzle, or just to coast a while. Enjoy these times. In our busy lives, there are few times when one can be alone. Make the most of these times.

4. The large bed pillows are comfortable for sleeping. Here's where the day ends and one takes stock of the day. A clean conscience is a "soft pillow." Hebrews 13:18 says, "We trust we have a good conscience, in all things willing to live honestly." Ephesians 4:26 says, "Let not the sun go down upon your wrath." To carry care to bed is to sleep with a pack on your back. "Casting all your care on him, for he careth for you" (1 Peter 5:7). This is the time to be thankful for your loved one, for the blessings of the day, for new friends made, for old friends already made, for work, for study, for problems and their solutions, for the challenge of the next day. You are comfortable!

5. Your arms are such handy pillows. These are your prayer pillows that you can use right now. Maybe something has broken your heart, maybe you have a problem too big for you. The Lord is there instantly! Psalm 27:1 tells us, "The Lord is my light and my salvation; whom shall I fear? The Lord is the strength of my life; of whom shall I be afraid?"

6. Sometimes you may have no pillow at all. There seems to be no answers, no help, and no place to get help. Sometimes the Lord lets you have hard times so you will rest completely in Him. Psalm 12:1 says, "Help, Lord"! That is all that is necessary for Him to hear you.

7. The "fun pillows" or accent pillows may be the most important. Your life together should have more smiles than tears, more happiness than

sorrow. You may have to smile through your tears at times. Your husband will need your smile, your merry heart. Proverbs 17:22 tells us "a merry heart doeth good like a medicine." Maybe your husband will do something you are not happy about, but remember, "a soft answer turneth away wrath" (Proverbs 15:1). A smile will help. Maybe the cooking doesn't turn out so great. Remember, "better is a dinner of herbs where love is, than a stalled ox and hatred therein" (Proverbs 15:17). A smile helps here, too! Take time to enjoy and have fun together, even if it is just taking a trip to a nearby drive-in for an ice cream cone.

8. Some pillows are real, some are not. Some love is real, some love is not. Real love has to be worked at all the time. You can't sail through and think you have your man. If you don't keep him loving you, someone else might! 1 Corinthians 13:4-7 sums up what real love is all about. Let's read it.

God's richest blessing be on you both as you step out together.

Show Love With a Hug

Scripture: "I have lent him to the Lord; as long as he liveth he shall be lent to the Lord" (1 Samuel 1:28).

Gift: Make a pillow center with counted cross-stitch. Pattern books usually have a design or two with the word *hug* in them. Make the pillow out of checked gingham.

Decorations: Have flower arrangements with bows of checked gingham.

Devotion:
When a new baby comes into a home, both parents learn in a hurry that they have a big job ahead of them. Here is a brand-new human being—created by God—with a life to be lived for eternity. You parents will mold this child for good or for bad. He will pick up many of your mannerisms, your speech, and even your thought patterns. Although your child is not a carbon copy or clone of you, he will be very much like both of you. That's awesome!

The first thing you should do as parents is to give your baby back to God. Remember the Old Testament story of Hannah, who prayed hard for a baby? When God answered her prayer and gave her baby Samuel, she willingly gave him back to God. Here is what she said: "For this child I prayed; and the Lord hath given me my petition which I asked of him: therefore also I have lent him to the Lord; as long as he liveth he shall be lent to the Lord" (1 Samuel 1:27, 28). When you give anything to God He gives back in abundance. This is true when you allow Him to have first place with your child. The blessings will be beyond measure. And they will continue through the years.

Proverbs 22:6 tells us to "train up a child in the way he should go: and when he is old, he will not depart from it." Oh, there will be many detours. There will be problems and heartaches, but with God's help the job gets done! Hang onto the Scriptures; spend time in prayer; claim God's promises, and He'll bring you through.

There will be thorns along the way. Your child will need to fall and get up again and again. Your child will have to face problems and learn to overcome them. That's the way we all grow. If you take a rose bush and cut off its thorns, the blossoms will fall off before they reach full bloom. Leave the thorns on and a beautiful rose will develop. The thorns in your child's life will help him develop into a worthwhile person.

Your example is important. Let your child see Christ and His Word in you. Read the Bible and teach your child its concepts. God told His people this when they were ready to enter the promised land: "These words, which I command thee this day, shall be in thine heart: and thou shalt teach them diligently unto thy children, and shalt talk of them when thou sittest in thine house, and when thou walkest by the way, and when thou liest down, and when thou risest up" (Deuteronomy 6:6, 7).

How do you treat guests in your home? Are they welcome? Are you interested in them? Is it a gossip session? Do you think you have to have your house spotless and prepare a gourmet meal before you entertain? Scrubbed floors, polished furniture, and fancy meals are not always necessary. Most folks really don't care if your home is ready for inspection. Coffee, soft drinks, popcorn, and peanut-butter sandwiches can be more fun than a fancy meal if there is genuine love. Your children will learn to love and care for others when they see you do this.

You've all seen the bumper stickers that say, "Have you hugged your child today?" Hugging is important. If you have ever watched any Special Olympics, you will remember the folks who are at the finish line, waiting for the runners to come in. Whether the runners win or lose, these people give them a big hug and tell them they did a great job. These folks are called "huggers." Learn to be "huggers." Everyone needs the kind touch of another human being. Babies especially need this contact. Without it they do not thrive.

Your new baby will be easy to love while he is tiny. Hugging will be natural. But when he grows a bit and is disobedient, you may have to remind yourself that he still needs your loving arms around him. Let him know you still love him, even though you don't love what he just did. God, our heavenly Father, loves us, yet does not love everything we do. Keep His example ever before you.

Some parents seem to show little affection to their children. The children, especially as they grow older, do not experience the hugs and kisses that are a natural result of affection between people who love each other. These children grow up to be cold, uncaring adults. If you want your child to be a warm, affectionate person, be that way with him when he is growing up. And remember, the more love you give to him, the more you will have. Isn't that great!

To have a happy, loving, giving child, first give him to God, then give him your love, and remember to show that love through plenty of hugs!

Reach Out

Scripture: "For the eyes of the Lord are over the righteous, and his ears are open unto their prayers" (1 Peter 3:12).

Gifts: A toy telephone for the baby to be. For the grandmothers, shrink-art plaques (see sketch).

Decorations: Have a variety of telephones, either real ones or toy ones, with perhaps some flowers arranged in the middle—either on the speaker's table or on the serving table.

Devotion:

> Reach out, reach out and touch someone;
> Reach out, reach out and just say, "Hi."

This familiar song is talking about using the phone, of course. But there are other ways to reach out. Babies do a lot of reaching out even though they are quite small. Have you ever thought about the many people your baby will reach out to, long before he or she is even able to walk or talk? And how those around your baby will respond to that reaching out!

God surely knew what He was doing when he planned for folk to start out life as babies. Can you imagine how it would be to acquire your family all grown up? Be thankful for little ones.

You probably realize by now that you have a big job ahead of you. You have a new life to mold, a life that will live through all eternity. Don't let this thought frighten you. You are not the first new mother! Many have been through it before, with the same worries and fears you are experiencing now.

> Relax, my dear. Your little elf
> Is just an amateur herself.
> So, if your hands, so newly filled
> With tasks, seem somewhat less than skilled,
> Relax, I say; this little pinkling
> Doesn't have the slightest inkling
> That you are new to baby lore;
> She never had a Mom before.[1]

You probably have had your home and family all under control. Now this new baby will change things. Your home will never be the same again. Neither will your life be the same. Babies reach out and touch, and leave their mark—whether it is on the wall, or in your heart!

You will have to learn to divide your time differently. You will have to make your husband understand that he has to share you with the baby. And you will have to learn to share his time with the baby too. Remember this, your love will grow as a new life comes into your home.

As your child reaches out, he will bring happiness to your family. Enjoy all of it. He will also bring problems and even unhappiness at times. Your heart will ache as only a mother's heart can. Let your husband share in the happy and unhappy times. Your child needs both of you. That's the way God planned families.

> Smaller than a tulip,
> Softer than a rose,
> But by love's secret miracle
> She has your eyes, my nose.
>
> Is it not a marvel
> How, with little fuss,
> God has kept since Genesis
> An exact blueprint of us?[2]

There are busy days ahead—a crying baby, diapers to wash, dinner to get, groceries to buy, the dentist to see, and company coming in. . . .

When you're through the day, settle down and be quiet. "Be still and know that I am God" (Psalm 46:10). If you find you are just too tired at night for prayer with God, get up a little earlier in the morning. You'll find it is the best time of the day.

Your baby will touch your friends. Invite your friends into your home. Let your baby learn to love and respect older folks and to know what kind of friends you have. And teach your child how to act with visitors. If a child has love and respect for Mom, for Dad, and for others, he will learn to love and respect God much easier.

Babies always touch grandparents' lives. The phone ad, "Reach out and touch someone," often pictures a grandparent talking to the child or the child's parent. Grandparents want to know how things are. They want to help. Listen to them; learn from them. Let your child learn from them as well.

Your child eventually will reach out and touch those he comes in contact with at church, at school, and even farther. Make sure that he or she is taught right from wrong, to love God and serve Him. Then the influence he has will be for good to all those he touches.

Yours and your husbands' lives will be touching your child every day. You will have to work every day toward living an upright life before your child. Remember, "children are a heritage of the Lord" (Psalm 127:3).

You do have a big job. Think about this:

> Some children walk the high road
> While others tread the low;
> A mother can determine
> Which way her child will go."[3]

Your home, your family, and your friends will be touched by this little one. Take time to pray, to learn, to love, and to enjoy. May the Lord bless you, as you reach out and touch others.

[1]Reprinted with permission from *Showers*, Rieman Publications, Inc., P.O. Box 643, Milwaukee, WI 53212.
[2]Ibid.

[3]Reprinted with permission from *The Log*, Haven of Rest, Hollywood, CA 90028.

Grandmothers Are Old-Fashioned

Scripture: "I call to remembrance the unfeigned faith that is in thee, which dwelt first in thy grandmother Lois, and thy mother Eunice; and I am persuaded that in thee also" (2 Timothy 1:5).

Gifts: An appropriate plaque or embroidered picture for the mother-to-be and small ones for the grandmothers.

Decorations: If possible, have some old-fashioned dolls on the speaker's table and/or serving table. Or use Raggedy Ann dolls and teddy bears, both of which have been popular for many years.

Devotion:

Grandmothers are old-fashioned. In fact, they date way back to Eve. Not only was Eve the first mother in the world, she was also the first grandmother. Did you ever think of that? No doubt she was excited over Cain's Enoch and Seth's Enos, especially since there had never been grandchildren before! And just think of the number of grandchildren she could have had. The Bible says that Adam lived eight hundred years after the birth of Seth and had sons and daughters. What a photograph album she could have had!

Yes, Grandmothers are old-fashioned. They have been around a long time. And what a heritage they give your baby!

Grandmothers, you have quite a responsibility! Don't let this frighten you, however, but think of it as an opportunity—a new little one to love and cherish and to teach. Are you familiar with all the Bible stories little ones can understand? If not, get out your Bibles and read. Look for some Bible storybooks that will help you teach those important Bible concepts to the new little one to come. Let him or her know that Jesus loves him, that God made him, and that he can talk to God and Jesus. He won't understand at first, but he will be eager to learn. And he will absorb your attitudes toward God and His Son Jesus. Timothy learned, not only from his mother, but from his grandmother. And the apostle Paul immortalized Lois because of this.

Grandmothers are great for mending torn pants, for hemming dresses, and sewing on buttons. And as they work on these, they often communicate with the little one whose "church dress" they are mending. If you have an opportunity to do this, take time to talk to and listen to that grandchild. She will soon be able to communicate a great deal to you if you let her.

Grandmothers are old-fashioned. After all, they are of the generation before you, mother-to-be. That's a long time ago. Babies are raised differently now. We've learned to be more relaxed, more adaptable with schedules. We've found out that babies are pretty hardy little individuals. But remember, grandmothers have had lots of experience. They have much to offer. Listen and learn from them.

Grandmothers always have pictures to show. Photo companies love grandmothers!

Grandmothers call a lot. Phone companies love them too!

Grandmothers are concerned. They are never quite convinced that you can rear that baby properly.

Grandmothers are always ready to tell anyone they meet about their grandchildren. It's best not to ask unless you mean to listen and have an hour of time!

Grandmothers are proud. There's no one quite like their grandchild or grandchildren. No one!

And here's how a grandchild feels about her grandmother:

I love to have my Grandma come,
She is so soft and warm.
When I am in my Granny's arms,
I cannot come to harm.
She knows so many old-time things
that Mother doesn't know.
I listen to her tales all day;
I hate to see her go.
There's candy in her pocketbook,
Sometimes a toy or two.
The day I see my Grandma come
I never can be blue.

—*author unknown*

Yes, Grandmother's arms are always outstretched and full of love. "Grandmotheritis" hits everyone who has the privilege to become a grandmother. It's wonderful!

Grandmothers, make the most of your opportunities. Love a lot, help where and when needed, pray for your grandchild and the parents, and enjoy that new baby! Remember, you are important.

Mother, humor those grandmothers. Teach your baby to love them. Teach your baby to respect them and enjoy being with them. They have much to offer. They are your baby's heritage.

First Steps

Scripture: "The steps of a good man are ordered by the Lord: and he delighteth in his way. . . . The law of his God is in his heart; none of his steps shall slide" (Psalm 37:23, 31).

Gift: Give the mother-to-be a pair of baby sneakers suitable for either a girl or a boy.

Decorations: Each table can have a different type of shoe with a flower arrangement in or with each.

Devotion:

Note: Have as visual aids the following shoes: booties or soft-soled baby shoes, hard-soled baby shoes, patent leather dress slippers, sneakers (any size), loafers, high-heeled shoes, bedroom slippers, and old, well-worn shoes.

After your baby is born, one of the first things you will do is to look him over from head to toe. You'll marvel at each small, perfect part of his anatomy. And how precious and beautiful will be his tiny feet! They'll be lovely to hold and to behold.

After a while, those little feet may not look quite so good to you when you find out the price of shoes! Your child will need many, many pairs of shoes of all kinds to protect his feet as he grows. Let's look at some examples.

The first foot coverings you will probably put on your little one will be booties, or perhaps soft-soled shoes. These are soft little foot coverings that keep baby warm and comfortable. And that's the way tiny babies like to feel. They enjoy being warm and you enjoy the warm feelings as they snuggle up to you. Babies usually wear these soft shoes until they take their first few steps. How exciting it is to watch these first steps and even count them. Not only do we count baby's steps, but listen to what Job said: "Doth not he see my ways, and count all my steps?" (31:4). God knows all about your baby's steps and even counts your steps!

Once a baby starts to walk he graduates to hard-soled shoes. These are usually awkward and difficult to get used to, and often hard to put on as baby grips his toes into a ball and keeps them that way. You have to work to get his toes spread out and then shove his foot into the shoe before he has time to curl those toes again. And sometimes Mom sort of "curls up her toes," not quite ready to give up and change her ways to fit those of her new infant. Eventually young families work all these things out and learn to adapt.

Hard-soled shoes are apt to be slick on the bottom at first. Sometimes we use a little sandpaper to roughen them or add some tape for a little roughness. How do we keep from sliding? God is our helper, according to Psalm 37:31: "The law of his God is in his heart; none of his steps shall slide." Isn't that a great promise?

Watch a little girl as she carefully walks in her first pair of patent leather slippers. She is careful not to scuff them and wants to show them to everyone. And just watch what happens if someone should dare step on them! These are important dress-up shoes. They are special.

Parents feel that their little girls are pretty special, too, as they dress up in their "Sunday best." They show them off and talk about them. Just let anyone hurt them and watch out! God is protective of His children too. He doesn't want anything bad to happen to them. Listen to David's words in Psalm 119:133: "Order my steps in thy word: and let not any iniquity have dominion over me." Let that be your prayer for your child and you.

Sneakers or tennis shoes are interesting shoes. They come in all sizes, colors, and fabrics. People from 6 months to 60 years wear them. They are for fun times—picnics, hiking, playing ball, climbing hills and fences, running, jumping, and skipping. They are practical. If they get soiled you just toss them in the washer.

Keep some fun in your life. Mothers often are the ones to teach a child to laugh. Laughter is so necessary in a child's life and as he grows older. Proverbs 17:22 says, "A merry heart doeth good like a medicine."

Loafers are for casual wear, for shopping, for watching a ball game, for taking a walk. You wear them for comfort and to be sure of your steps. Psalm 37:23 tells us that God orders our steps. "The steps of a good man are ordered by the Lord; and he delighteth in his way." Teach your child to trust in God so He will order his or her steps too.

Then there comes the day when your daughter wants her first pair of high heels. These are for dress-up times—dates, going to church, and special occasions. High heels are a bit tipsy, and girls need to practice walking in them so they won't fall and lose their dignity. Even though your daughter may have practiced wearing your heels through the years, her own are different. This is a symbol of growing up, of maturity. And with maturity comes discipline. If you have done your part through the years, exercising the necessary discipline, your child will have developed self-discipline by now. This is part of God's plan for families. In Genesis 18:19, God told Abraham He could become a great and mighty nation "for I know him, that he will command his children and his household after him, and they shall keep the way of the Lord." God is pleased when we do our part in preparing our children for life.

Bedroom slippers are comfortable and warm. They are often worn when we want to relax, to be satisfied, to be loved. Your home should be as comfortable and relaxing as a pair of bedroom slippers. Make it inviting and warm, a place for love. Make it a place where your child will want to bring his or her friends. Make it a peaceful place, without strife and bickering. If there is no peace at home, your child will not want to spend time there, and you'll lose him at an early age.

The last foot covering we want to talk about is an old shoe. This is the shoe that is comfortable because it has been molded to fit your foot. It gives and bends in just the right places. You are going to be molding your child so he or she will fit into your family and then into the world around us. Your example will have more influence than anything you can say. Your best guidebook is God's Word. Your best helper is the Lord. Proverbs 16:9 says, "The Lord directeth his steps." Make sure that you allow God to direct your steps so that your child can follow in those steps. Your child will then be following God.

This could be adapted to fit a women's retreat or a mother/daughter banquet. You might want musical selections between the talks on the different shoes. The program could be called "Come, Follow Me."

Lessons Seen in a Mirror

Scripture: "If any be a hearer of the word, and not a doer, he is like unto a man beholding his natural face in a glass: for he beholdeth himself, and goeth his way, and straightway forgetteth what manner of man he was" (James 1:23).

Gifts: Give each woman a small pocket mirror at the end of the message.

Decorations: If you want, prepare a very large decorated frame made of cardboard that the speaker can stand behind.

Devotion:

No matter how casually or elaborately you dressed today, you all probably used one item—a mirror. Even though you may have taken only a quick look at yourself, you looked into that mirror. There are two kinds of mirrors we want to talk about today.

The first is a dirty mirror. There are some things all dirty mirrors have in common. Here they are:

1. A dirty mirror comes gradually. It doesn't get dirty overnight. You usually don't even notice that it is getting dirty until you run your finger over it.

2. A dirty mirror comes easily. You don't have to work at getting a mirror dirty. Some get dusty—all by themselves. Your bathroom mirror gets water spots—and you don't even have to work to put them there.

3. A dirty mirror is easy to forget. While you are using your mirror you realize it needs cleaning, then you walk away from it and promptly forget it needs your attention.

4. Sometimes you have help getting a mirror dirty. If you have preschool children or grandchildren, you know what I mean!

5. Sometimes you just don't want to see that dirt on the mirror. A mirror that is in a place where it is seldom seen can be ignored for a long time.

James compares a man who hears God's Word but does not do anything about it to a man who looks in the mirror, notices that he needs something, but goes on about his life, forgetting what he saw.

How is your life like that dirty mirror?

1. It comes gradually. You start out clean as a new Christian, then gradually pick up sin here and there. You go back to your old habits, you lose your enthusiasm, your love for the Lord—gradually.

2. It comes easily. You become careless, you quit trying, you let down your standards, and you don't even have to work at it!

3. It is easy to forget. You say and do the things you used to do because you forget to live the way God wants you to.

4. Sometimes you have help. That help may come from old friends who are not Christians, or even through Christian friends who are willing to listen to gossip, and who do not encourage you to do what is right.

5. You don't want to see your dirt—your sinful nature. You begin to feel comfortable living the way you please, and you don't want to be reminded of what God expects of you. Above all, you don't read His Word, for it can quickly point out your sins. Listen to these Scriptures. Psalm 14:3: "They are all together become filthy." Romans 3:12: "They are together become unprofitable." Isaiah 64:6: "All our righteousnesses are as filthy rags."

How can you be like a clean mirror? How can you do a better job so you won't have to be ashamed of your life? In Acts 4, after the rulers had asked Peter and John about the healing of the lame man, the Scriptures say, "When they saw the boldness of Peter and John, and perceived that they were unlearned and ignorant men, they marveled; and they took knowledge of them, that they had been with Jesus" (v. 13).

Do you show Christ through your life as Peter and John did? Can others tell you have "been with Jesus"? Christ can't be seen through a life filled with sin. Only through a life that's clean, upright, and one that is lived close to God can others see Jesus. You need a daily "washing" in the Word and in prayer.

> You are writing a gospel, a chapter each day
> By things that you do and words that you say,
> Men read what you write, whether faithless or true.
> Say, what is the gospel according to *you*?
> —*author unknown*

There are three "T's" in our lives that need to be under control. They are a troublesome trio, at times difficult to tame. The Lord is the only One who can help. You don't dare start without Him.

Thought

Read Matthew 7:1-5. What do you think about? Are you critical all the time? Or, do you try to find something good in others, or in a given situation? How much praising of the Lord do you do?

Read James 4:13-15. Do you leave the future with the Lord? Yesterday is gone; you can't do anything about it. Tomorrow isn't here; you can't do much with it either. Today you have; praise the Lord for it!

Read Matthew 6:25-34. Concern or worry does not empty tomorrow of its sorrow, but it does empty today of its strength. Someone gave this prescription for the cure of worry. You'll find it works.

Talk to six folks today. Do not mention your concern. You'll find others have much bigger cares than you do and you can say, "Thank You, Lord!" for yours.

Temper

Read Genesis 4:1-8. There was temper and anger in the first book of the Bible, in the first family.

The result of anger without self-control is temper! Listen to what the Bible says about anger. "He that is soon angry dealeth foolishly" (Proverbs 14:17). "An angry man stirreth up strife, and a furious man aboundeth in transgression" (Proverbs 29:22). "Be not hasty in thy spirit to be angry: for anger resteth in the bosom of fools" (Ecclesiastes 7:9).

Has this ever happened to you? You made a big fuss over something you didn't like, then, when you think back on it later, you can't even remember what you were fussing about! But what damage you probably did by losing your temper!

Wouldn't you like to be like those who can keep quiet and not always stir the waters? This takes self-control!

Tongue

Read James 3:2-10. James describes our tongues so correctly. Your tongue tells everyone what your thoughts are. How revealing! "Those things which proceed out of the mouth come forth from the heart; and they defile the man. For out of the heart proceed evil thoughts, murders, adulteries, fornications, thefts, false witness, blasphemies" (Matthew 15:18, 19).

Use your tongue to praise God, and to build up those who are around you. May your prayer be, "Let the words of my mouth, and the meditation of my heart, be acceptable in thy sight, O Lord, my strength, and my redeemer" (Psalm 19:14).

A dirty or clean mirror—which will you be? A careless individual or one who is on fire for Christ—which one? Make sure, that as others look at you, they see Christ.

Bells, Bells, Bells

Scripture: "The trial of your faith, being much more precious than of gold that perisheth, though it be tried with fire, might be found unto praise and honor and glory at the appearing of Jesus Christ: whom having not seen, ye love; in whom, though now ye see him not, yet believing, ye rejoice with joy unspeakable and full of glory: receiving the end of your faith, even the salvation of your souls" (1 Peter 1:7-9).

Gifts: Have an inexpensive bell for each lady present.

Decorations: Arrange a display of bells on a table near the speaker's stand. Have as many of the bells mentioned here as possible. Hold these up as you talk about them. The silent or tongueless bell is an inexpensive bell from which you have removed the clapper. The wagging-tongue bell is one that has had the clapper made longer so that it does not ring.

Devotion:

Many bells are made from substances that originally mixed with others under the earth's surface. Unless these substances were mixed, they were useless and impure.

Until you accept the Lord as your personal Savior, you are impure and useless as far as God's kingdom is concerned. This applies to everyone, for "all have sinned and come short of the glory of God" (Romans 3:23).

45

Those who work with this material to make bells must have the proper tools. God also needs a special tool to work on our hearts to make us useful. That tool is the Holy Spirit, and He works through the Word of God. "Is not my word like as a fire? saith the Lord; and like a hammer that breaketh the rock in pieces?" (Jeremiah 23:29). The hardest heart can be softened by the Holy Spirit.

No amount of raw materials and tools will make a bell that rings until that bell has been refined or fired. We, too, are refined through trials and temptations. *(Read the Scripture given at the beginning of this message.)*

Metal bells are made by pouring the molten substance into molds. The mold is often broken after the bell is cast. Our mold is Jesus Christ. Our lives must be made to conform to His if we are to be useful to Him. Our mold, too, was broken. "This is my body, which is broken for you" (1 Corinthians 11:24).

Bells that are misshapen, that crack in firing, that do not completely conform to their molds are useless. They are cast aside. This too applies to us. When we refuse to conform, when we refuse to obey, we are useless. We will someday be cast aside.

Let's look at some specific bells and see what they can teach us.

School Bell: This bell was rung by hand. It was loud enough to be heard in the farthest corner of the school playground.

Some of us may be like this bell—not timid, but clear and loud. God wants us to speak out for Him.

Cowbells: These bells are not particularly melodious but they are very useful and necessary. They let the farmer know just where his flock is.

Many Christians are like a cowbell—useful and necessary. They may not work where you can see and hear them, but they are there, working in the background, doing their part.

Sleigh Bells: These bells are always used in numbers. They work well together.

How important it is for Christians to learn to work well together. We can't all be soloists in the choir, or lead teacher of a class. But we can learn to work well with others who are trying to please God.

A Noisy Bell: Some bells make a lot of noise but they are not very pretty to look at or to hear.

Christians may find that they are making a lot of noise without really accomplishing a great deal except to get on people's nerves. Make sure that you ring with a purpose for God.

A Quiet-sounding Bell: This is a bell that doesn't make a big show, but may serve a specific purpose.

Some people go quietly about their business of serving the Lord, making as little show as possible. They do what they can for the Lord and do it willingly.

Swiss Bells: These are large, strong bells. They are like people who are strong in the Lord. These people seem to roll with the punches, always coming out on top. This takes great faith, patience, and love for the Lord.

A Tinkling Bell: This is a happy-sounding bell. It reminds us of a Christian who goes around with a smile on his face and a song in his heart. He praises the Lord, even if things don't go just right. And he can do so much good by helping others to be cheerful.

A Broken Bell: Some bells break and can no longer be used. There is no bell for this lesson because a broken bell is cast out. Take a lesson from this and make sure you are not a broken bell, useless to God.

Tongueless Bell: This bell looks pretty, but it cannot be rung. It is just for ornamentation. Unless you can tell the good news about Jesus, you are of no more use to God than is a tongueless bell.

A Wagging-tongue Bell: Here you can see plenty of action, but no sound. Do you know some people like this? They talk a lot but they say little, if anything, of value. They talk about the weather, the news, about other folks, but never about the gospel. Make sure that you are not just a wagging-tongue bell!

A Cracked Bell: This bell looks pretty from the outside, but it has no tone. When we allow sin to enter our lives, we too may look good on the outside, but we are no longer useful to God. We cannot "ring" for Him. But He has promised to forgive us when we come back to Him. Read 1 John 1:9.

A Pretty, Clear-ringing Bell: This bell is beautiful on the outside, and it sounds beautiful when rung. It does what a bell should do! A faithful, active Christian is like this. Her life is beautiful to look upon, and she is working diligently for her Lord. She is doing what is expected of her. This is what we must strive for—to be pure within, clear in our testimony, and full of praise for God and care for others.

The Wedding Bell: Last, but not least, this beautiful wedding bell reminds us of the wedding supper of the Lamb. "Blessed are they which are called unto the marriage supper of the Lamb" (Revelation 19:9). Who are invited to this supper? Jesus said, "Whosoever will, let him take the water of life freely" (Revelation 22:17). You have been invited. Have you accepted?

No matter what shape or of what material a bell may be made, it can have a purpose. We, too, can be useful to God, no matter what we look like, what our age is, what our talents are. We have been made in the image of God to serve Him. Let's do so with all our strength and might!

Think and Thank

Scripture: "Be careful for nothing; but in every thing by prayer and supplication with thanksgiving let your requests be made known unto God. And the peace of God, which passeth all understanding, shall keep your hearts and minds through Christ Jesus. Finally, brethren, whatsoever things are true, whatsoever things are honest, whatsoever things are just, whatsoever things are pure, whatsoever things are lovely, whatsoever things are of good report; if there be any virtue, and if there be any praise, think on these things" (Philippians 4:6-8).

Gifts: Have an appropriate bookmark for each woman.

Decorations: An arrangement of seasonal flowers is sufficient. If you have a plaque or picture of "Praying Hands," or a picture of Jesus in prayer, put this in a focal point.

Devotion:
(Read Philippians 4:6-8 to begin your message. Do this yourself, or preferably, have someone else read it.)
You have all probably heard of companies that have "think tanks." These are comfortable rooms where company personnel can go to be quiet and think. As Christians, however, we know we should do more than think. We must also thank the Lord for His goodness toward us. Paul said in Philippians 4:6, "In every thing by prayer and supplication with thanksgiving let your requests be made known unto God."

49

THINK about a problem and all its side effects. Write this down. Take it to the Lord. Leave it there.

THANK the Lord for the problem, "giving thanks always for all things unto God and the Father in the name of our Lord Jesus Christ" (Ephesians 5:20). Thank Him for the answers that are on the way. (Be ready for the answer. It may not be what you expect!)

THINK about your uninteresting day. All folk have them from time to time.

THANK the Lord that you're alive. Find someone to say thank-you to for some kindness done in the past. How about the grocery clerk, the minister, the mailman, the paper boy, a family member? These people will enjoy being told they've done a good job. Philippians 1:3 says, "I thank my God upon every remembrance of you." If your day is uninteresting, at least make someone else's interesting!

THINK of someone you can help today. You say, "I can't get out and do very much." Use your phone to keep in touch. How blest we are to be able to check with friends and see how they are without having to leave our homes. Perhaps you can tell a friend some piece of happy news. Have you ever thought of keeping in touch with a young mother? Maybe she's been cooped up all week with sick children. A word of encouragement would help her get through the day. If you can run errands, you can always find someone who needs a ride, some groceries, or a short visit. THANK the Lord for the phone or for your car and that you are able to help. Ephesians 4:32 says, "Be ye kind one to another, tender-hearted." You will feel good after you have helped someone. The days slip by so quickly. Use each one to its fullest.

THINK, "I'm having trouble sleeping." You wake up and can't go back to sleep. You wonder, "Why am I awake?"

THANK the Lord for this special time. You have no interruptions, no phone calls, no noise, no radio or TV. Maybe the Lord nudged you awake. Maybe He wanted to talk to you or maybe you needed to talk to Him. Read Psalm 103:1-5. Verse 4 says, "Who crowneth thee with lovingkindness and tender mercies." Instead of counting sheep or troubles, list all the good things God has done for you. You'll soon be asleep.

THINK, "I'm not important."

THANK the Lord that there is only one of you! Just think how important you are. Psalm 103:4 says, "He knoweth our frame." There never was, is, or will be another just like you! You are made for something special. You have a work to do and no one else can ever do it. You are "fearfully and wonderfully made." You are important in God's eyes.

THINK of Calvary.
THANK and praise the Lord for His gift to us. John 3:16 says, "For God so loved the world, that he gave his only begotten Son, that whosoever believeth in him should not perish, but have everlasting life." Thank God for that kind of love for us.

THINK of Easter.
THANK and praise God that Jesus is risen! Mark 16:6 tells us, "He saith unto them, Be not affrighted: ye seek Jesus of Nazareth, which was crucified: he is risen; he is not here: behold the place where they laid him." Our salvation is complete. Isn't that marvelous!

THINK of the forgiveness of Christ.
THANK the Lord that He will forgive us. "If we confess our sins, he is faithful and just to forgive us our sins, and to cleanse us from all unrighteousness" (1 John 1:9). Oh, the sweet peace He gives after forgiveness!

THINK that something great is going to happen today.
THANK Him for His Word; then for His care for you today. Read all of Psalm 121.

(Close by reading Philippians 4:6-8 again.)

Sowing Seeds

Scripture: "He which soweth sparingly shall reap also sparingly; and he which soweth bountifully shall reap also bountifully" (2 Corinthians 9:6).

Gifts: Have a packet of seeds for each woman present.

Decorations: Have posters of fruits, vegetables, and flowers, if possible. Also, a child-size set of garden implements can be used along with some flowers or an arrangement of fresh vegetables on the refreshment table or speaker's table.

Devotion:

Once there was a woman who had trouble cooking and baking. It was not her best talent! Her husband and son just never knew what to expect at mealtime. She could usually, however, bake good bread. One day she changed her recipe for bread. As she mixed the dough, she just knew she had something good here! She set the dough aside to rise.

After about thirty minutes, the dough had not changed. The woman set it in warm water, but it didn't change. Then she put the dough by the warm furnace, but it still didn't rise.

Finally she decided to get rid of the dough. She took it to the garden and buried it! She promptly forgot about it. Winter came. Spring came. It was time for her son to work up the garden for Spring planting. After a while, her son came in and said, "I've found the biggest mushroom in the garden!"

Everyone went to see the mushroom. Yes, you've guessed it. Right where she had buried the bread dough, was the mushroom! The sun had activated the yeast!

Her husband, with a wink, said, "I'll get the plow and plow the garden now. Mom, will you go in and start some cinnamon rolls?"[1]

This story has several lessons in it. What verses or stories in the Bible does it remind you of? *(Let women answer).* "What you sow, so shall you reap," "Be sure your sins will find you out," the story of Ananias and Sapphira.

(Have someone read Galatians 6:7-9 and Acts 5:1-11.)

Spring is almost here. What do you think about when you hear the word *Spring?*

—Mud! (It has to get worse before it gets better!)

—The days are getting warmer and longer.

—Spring housecleaning must be done—scrubbing, painting, picking up outside, washing windows, and so forth.

—Gardens need to be prepared.

No matter what the age of the person, everyone gets excited and enthused about gardening in the Spring! Everyone wants to look at the seed catalog. Everyone wants to get out and get the feel of the earth and to plan the garden.

The ground is tilled and the seeds are planted. You have a few warm days. Everyone watches for that first green shoot to come from the ground. Sometimes you can't tell whether that green shoot is a plant or a weed. (Sometimes it looks like you are cultivating weeds in your garden!) You watch the weather reports, hoping there won't be a frost to freeze the beans and corn. (In your excitement, you always plant too early!)

New growth is so much fun to watch. First comes that tiny shoot, then the first and second leaves, and soon the vines are running over the ground and up fences, only it's nothing like the seed you thought you planted!

But, there are problems. If the garden is worked too early it gets hard. The plants can't get through. Jesus talked about this in Mark 4:5, 6.

Sometimes it rains and rains. The seeds rot or are washed away or the ground develops a hard crust on top.

Or a frost comes along and kills everything. It is never as much fun to plant the garden a second time!

Then there are the weeds. They are the biggest problem you must face. After a while, you just let them go, or pull only enough to get by.

And, sometimes, you quit! Isn't that the easy way out?

Finally comes the harvest. You get tomatoes for tomatoes, onions for onions, and so forth. But your harvest will be small if the ground is hard, if it's too wet, if there's a late frost, or if there are too many weeds, OR, if you didn't sow enough seeds!

Then there are the gardens worked on by faithful gardeners from early morning until late afternoon. These gardeners hoe, rototill, fertilize, pat down, dig up, transplant, pull weeds, hoe some more, put plastic down, water, the whole bit. And aren't their gardens beautiful!

Let's make some comparisons between gardens and the Christian life. What does all this mean to us?

We could compare the Spring gardening excitement to the excitement and enthusiasm of a new Christian. When you first became a Christian you wanted to tell everyone, especially your friends. You couldn't understand why they weren't as excited as you were.

You had many new duties and obligations to perform as a new Christian. (Of course, you considered them privileges.) You began to read the Bible—you'd never done that before. You told others about Jesus—

you'd never done that either. You prayed—you'd never done that except on rare occasions when something was terribly wrong!

No matter what age a person is when he or she becomes a Christian, there is great excitement and enthusiasm. And other Christians enjoy watching you grow. They are even willing to help you learn and grow. They are pleased to see you make changes in your life—perhaps your speech, your dress, your habits, even your friends.

After a while, however, you are on your own. It is up to you whether you will go on growing or just sit back and rest. Temptations and discouragements, like weeds, creep in. You have to work hard to keep going. And sometimes, you quit!

Then comes the harvest. Yes, there will be a harvest for Christians, as well as for seeds. What have you done with your time, your money, your talents? Have you brought other souls to God? Were you willing to give of your time to help others? How about your money? Did you give willingly? Did you really get involved when your friend or neighbor was struggling? Were you critical of others? How bountifully did you sow?

There should be beautiful fruits in your harvest, not weeds. What would your harvest be like if you had to reap today?

Of course, there are many who work from early morning to late at night living the Christian life. What a testimony they are for everyone. What an example! Their harvest is joyous, peaceful, pleasing, comforting, and so rewarding!

Remember the words in 2 Corinthians 9:6—"He which soweth sparingly shall reap also sparingly; and he which soweth bountifully shall reap also bountifully."

(Read Galatians 6:7-9 again.)

[1]Reprinted with permission of *Farm Wife News*, P.O. Box 643, Milwaukee, WI 53201.

Thoughts for Mothers

Scripture: "Train up a child in the way he should go: and when he is old, he will not depart from it" (Proverbs 22:6).

Gifts: An inexpensive plaque or bookmark for each woman, or a small potted plant.

Decorations: Baskets of flowers or branches of Spring shrubs.

Devotion:

Do you know that you are in a business—the business of being a mother? Have you ever thought about that? Have you looked over your business lately, or have you overlooked it? You must take stock or inventory once in a while. No other business can go very long without doing so.

The sad thing is, you as a mother make mistakes. Sometimes you think other things are more important than training your children. You can get so busy working away from and at home, that you can't see what is happening. How long has it been since you sat and talked with your child, in spite of the dishes or laundry that awaited you? Do you know your child's plans for tomorrow, for next week, for next year? Or do you know those plans only when they are dropped on you so suddenly you have no time to talk to the Lord about them? Proverbs 29:15 says, "A child left to himself bringeth his mother to shame."

A mother is concerned, from the first time she sees her new baby, that it is physically perfect and healthy. She makes sure the baby eats just the right foods, gets adequate rest, has the proper toys, and wears the latest fashions. Of course you want your child to be healthy and look good. You want him to excel at everything, to participate in sports, in school, and in community activities. This is as it should be. But sometimes a mother becomes so obsessed with the physical well-being of her child that she neglects the spiritual side.

But what about the spiritual life of the child? How important is it? When should a mother begin a child's spiritual training? As soon as she begins his physical care! Don't wait until he is "old enough" to go to church. He is old enough as soon as he is able to go anywhere. Parents who take their children to Sunday school and church from the time they are born are training their children in the importance of consistent attendance and worship.

Think about this poem:

Mary had a little boy, his soul was white as snow;
He never went to Sunday school, 'cause Mary wouldn't go.
He never heard the tales of Christ that thrilled the childish mind;
While other children went to class, this child was left behind.
And as he grew from babe to youth, she saw to her dismay
A soul that once was snowy white became a dingy gray.
Realizing he was lost, she tried to win him back,
But now, the soul that once was white had turned to ugly black.
She even started back to church, and Bible study too.
She begged the preacher, "Isn't there a thing that you can do?"
The preacher tried—failed and said, "We're just too far behind.
I tried to tell you years ago, but you would pay no mind!"
And so, another soul is lost, that once was white as snow.
Sunday school could have helped, but Mary wouldn't go.

—author unknown

Don't wait until it is too late.

Parents who are faithful in serving the Lord are teaching by their actions. What does your child see? Do you really care? Has your child made a decision to accept the Lord as his Savior? Have you ever talked to him or her about this most important decision? Remember, your children are the only things you can take to Heaven!

Do you think your children do what you tell them, or do what they see you do? Listen to them as they play. Sounds like a tape recording, doesn't it—a tape recording of you! Is your child seeing Christ in your everyday life? Ezekiel 16:44 says, "As is the mother, so is her daughter."

How much time do you spend praying with your children? This is a big responsibility. If you don't set the example and teach them to pray, they may never learn to talk to God and depend upon Him. Have you taught your children to repeat rhyming sentences, or to really talk to God? (We don't talk to our friends on earth in memorized rhymes; why should we talk to God that way?) When have your children heard you talk to God?

Teach your child to obey you and have respect for you and for other adults. A child who has not been taught to respect and obey adults will not learn to respect and obey God. Paul instructed parents to bring their children up in the nurture and admonition of the Lord. He told children to "obey your parents in the Lord: for this is right" (Ephesians 6:1).

Solomon gave some good advice to parents when he said in Proverbs 22:5, "Foolishness is bound in the heart of a child; but the rod of correction shall drive it far from him." The Lord made our anatomy with a "back porch" for a purpose. He also said, in Ephesians 6:4, "Fathers, provoke not your children to wrath." One good spanking goes a long way! Don't overdo this.

Take stock of your business. See how good a business manager you are. Are you setting the example in consistent church attendance and service, in prayer, in respect, and in honoring God? As a Christian mother, make your motto that of Joshua's—"As for me and my house, we will serve the Lord" (24:15).

May also be used for a mother/daughter banquet.

Ring the Bells!

Scripture: "She brought forth her firstborn son, and wrapped him in swaddling clothes, and laid him in a manger; because there was no room for them in the inn" (Luke 2:7).

Gifts: Give each woman something inexpensive but appropriate to the season, such as a small container of homemade candy, a religious tree ornament, or a felt sock with a candy cane in it.

Decorations: Anything appropriate to the season, but with a sacred emphasis.

Devotion:

(Have someone ready to sing "Ring the Bells" at the end of your message.)

When you think of Christmas, what comes to mind? *(Give the women several minutes to share.)* A number of years ago, there was a man-on-the-street program. Several people were asked that question. Here are some of their answers:

—hustle and bustle

—the family, all coming to dinner

—no money left

—presents to buy

No one said a thing about the birth of Jesus. What should have come to their minds?

—Christ the Lord

—Immanuel, "God with us"

—songs and carols

—the star and the Wise-men

—sharing with family and friends

—bells

All of these are part of Christmas, aren't they.

Think for a minute about some of the things we do at Christmas:

—Bake cookies. Trying new recipes along with the old favorites is fun. Letting the children help is a good experience for them.

—Send cards. What a good way to remember old friends and keep in touch. It is also a means of witnessing to those who do not know God and His Son.

—Clean house. Whether you do it to get ready for company, or because it is Jesus' birthday, it is a part of the holiday. Playing Christmas records helps to make the work easier. So does having the whole family help.

—Family gatherings. What a happy time for families to be together! And what traditions are developing as you get together each year!

—Trim the tree. This and other decorations are an important part of the season. Make sure that some of your decorations say that it is Jesus' birthday.

—Christmas programs. These are so delightful and something to remember for years to come. And no one knows the good that will come from them as the groundwork is laid for the future. Many children, and parents, hear the story of Jesus' birth for the first time at a Christmas program, either put on by children or by adults.

Your first Christmas together as husband and wife was very special. You'll always remember it.

Then there's your child's first Christmas. How precious! How many pictures you took! How excited you were! (More excited than baby was!)

Having a baby of your own probably made you think about Mary and her Baby. Your baby was born in a nice clean, comfortable hospital. Her's was born in a cold, dark stable. You rushed to the hospital in a modern automobile. She either rode a donkey, or more probably, walked.

The family "flutter" that was caused by the birth of your baby was very different from the heavenly "flutter" for Mary's Son. Luke 2:16, 17 tells of the rejoicing of the angels and shepherds.

Your baby came as a mortal. Mary's came as the Savior. In fact, He came to be your child's Savior, as well as your own. "For unto you is born this day in the city of David a Saviour, which is Christ the Lord" (Luke 2:11). Praise the Lord! Your baby can live because Mary's baby came to die. He was the ransom not only for you and your child, but for all mankind. "God commendeth his love toward us, in that, while we were yet sinners, Christ died for us" (Romans 5:8).

In Mexico City, several years ago at Christmastime, the folk there used the government buildings around a city square to proclaim the birth of Christ. With the use of colored lights, they showed the life of Christ from His birth to His resurrection. When the lights were turned on, there was a hush. Then a large bell in a nearby church began to ring. It was a thrilling time for those who were there. Even today there is a "flutter" when we think of the gift of salvation that was given that first Christmas.

The great bell in Mexico City pealed out the good news of Jesus' birth. Wouldn't it be wonderful if all church buildings had bells! They could proclaim His resurrection at Easter. They could proclaim the happiness over one soul that is saved. And they could proclaim that Jesus is coming again.

Ring the bells, oh, ring the bells to tell the good news! And let us be thankful for Jesus, who is the good news!

(Have soloist sing "Ring the Bells" to conclude the program.)

Little Girls, Big Girls

Scripture: "Many daughters have done virtuously, but thou excellest them all" (Proverbs 31:29).

Gifts: A ribbon butterfly for each mother and daughter.

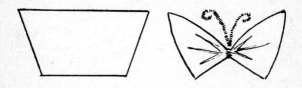

Decorations: A collection of dolls would be interesting. Have modern ones, and some old-fashioned ones if possible. Place a doll on each table with, perhaps, a ruffle of nylon net around it.

Devotion:

There is nothing in the world quite like a little girl! She is an enigma. She can be a loving "mommy" to her dolls one minute and throw them down and play with trucks and cars the next. She can get so dirty you hardly recognize her, yet respond to soap and water to become the pinkest, prettiest little rose you ever laid eyes on!

A little girl can electrify a room by just slipping in and laughing in her ripple of joy. She can be the most poised little lady one minute and the next she can be standing on her head.

When she cries, she cries all over. Everyone knows she's doing it. Then she can giggle all over. It may be caused by a lick on her face from her kitty, a funny song, or a humpy worm.

A little girl can melt the heart of the man she calls Daddy by just saying, "I love you," then turn around and refuse to obey him when he tells her to go to bed.

A little girl can run like the wind when a friend is calling, but can slow down to a turtle-pace when Mommy wants her to help.

She loves ducks, kittens, turtles, Mom, birthdays, and presents, and hates icky worms, spinach, and picking up her toys.

A little girl has the faith in God that just expects answers to her prayers.

Little girls soon grow up to be bigger girls, almost overnight, it seems.

An older girl can holler like a banshee if a younger brother gets into her things, but she will stand to the last if someone should hurt or take advantage of him five minutes later.

You can't get her to go to bed at night, and then you can't move her till nearly noon the next day.

While she can make the best cookies ever, she can also make the biggest mess in the kitchen.

Blue jeans, shirts, and sweaters are her uniform, yet she loves to dress in a frilly dress, looks like a princess in it, and loves every minute she's wearing it.

She can remember all your mistakes, the time you were supposed to be somewhere at a certain time, and your going the wrong way on a one-way street. But she can forget to say thank-you, where she left her shoes, to brush her hair, or what she was supposed to get for you from the other room!

A girl loves spaghetti, pizza, root beer, and ice cream, and hates eggs, carrots, and soup with a passion.

A girl loves to go somewhere—anywhere! She loves new shoes and old sweatshirts. She hates to wipe the dishes, to pick up her things, and to sweep the porch.

Then, overnight, that girl turns into a young lady, and before you know it, she'll have a little girl of her own.

All girls are beautiful in their own way. They make God's world a better place. Little girls are special. Big girls, while hard to get along with, are impossible to get along without.

Though a mother may have many daughters, each one is special, and each one "excellest them all."

The prayer of each Christian mother should be that her daughter will be loving, sweet, kind, pure, and above all, one who has a deep love for her Savior, Jesus Christ.

*This devotion can also be used for a father/daughter banquet by simply using "father" in place of "mother."

Boys Come in All Sizes

Scripture: "My son, despise not the chastening of the Lord; neither be weary of his correction: for whom the Lord loveth he correcteth; even as a father the son in whom he delighteth" (Proverbs 3:11, 12).

Gifts: Key chains with a Christian motto, or something else inexpensive yet masculine.

Decorations: Toy cars and trucks around arrangements of dried grass or something else not too fancy.

Devotion:

Have you praised the Lord for that bit of perpetual motion you call a son? Doesn't he keep you on your toes, no matter what his age! And if you don't have a boy in your home, go to a home that does, or ask a little boy into your home so you can experience this phenomenon.

Your little boy is the smartest, the cutest, and the funniest there is, anywhere in the world! He can ask more questions in fifteen minutes than you can answer in a day. And he can think of more reasons for climbing that forbidden ladder or tree, for going into the muddy garden, and for going next door than anyone on earth!

A little boy delights in Grandma's chocolate chip cookies, in Grandpa's tractor rides, and Dad's favorite tools. He loves baby ducks, mud puddles, little cars and tractors, and the noise of dragsters.

A ride in a big truck is the closest thing to Heaven, and right then he wants to be a truck driver when he grows up. (The same holds true of a firetruck and fireman, a tractor and farmer, and a train and engineer.)

He will work hard for most anyone—except his own mom and dad.

The noise that comes out of that wee kid at the most unexpected times is unbelievable!

He can be the most lovable, most cooperative, and the kindest little person—that is, when he is not being the most stubborn, the most cantankerous, and the biggest tease!

Little guys grow up to be big guys who like baseball, riding bikes with the gang, and teasing girls.

Sleep and eating vegetables are just not included in big boys' requirements for living. Neither are baths and girls—at least for a while.

A big boy can lose his shoes, his cap, his books, and anything else that is important—to you. Yet he knows exactly where he put his baseball glove and bat.

He can love his dog to death, but fight with his sister like a banty rooster.

Boys idolize sports figures, from high-school stars to the pros, and imitate them whether they are worthy of imitation or not.

And then one day, that boy begins to wash his face, comb his hair, and tuck in his shirt, and you know he is growing up. Now he knows that girls are something special, not to be teased and punched. He can't wait to get his driver's license. His voice goes up and down at odd moments.

With a teenage boy in the house, you suddenly find out how little you know. And if you don't realize it, he will point out this fact to you.

He is the "spittin' image" of his dad and you can already see what a fine young man he'll be in a few years—if you can just get through those years!

What a powerhouse! And you have to tame, shape, and mold him. He needs you to set limits, to enforce rules, to guide him. But you don't have to do all this alone. The Lord made this boy and He'll help you rear him, if you but ask. Your son may resent your discipline, at times, just as we resent God's ways. But remember, "whom the Lord loveth he correcteth; even as a father the son in whom he delighteth."

What would the world be like without little boys? without big boys? Empty! They put the sparkle, the power, and the fun in your life. Thank You, Lord, for boys!

This may also be used for a mother/son banquet.

More programs —
Motivational programs —
Programs to minister
to your women's group:

A Year of Programs for Today's Women
—featuring 12 outstanding women of the past
#2975

A glance into history reveals many women whose lives can be an inspiration to women today—women who challenged the standards of their day and brought about changes that affect us still.

Twelve such women are the basis for the twelve programs contained in this book. Their historical example supports the Biblical concept in each presentation, and provides material that is motivational, educational, and often humorous. These group-participation presentations will encourage the women in your group to be doers in life, rather than spectators only.

14 Women's Programs
—Making Your House a Home

#2974

Women who build homes require special tools and special knowledge of how to use them. Share programs with your women's group that teach them to use tools like love, loyalty, creativity, and prayer.

The skits, dialogues, panel discussions, etc., in this book require the involvement of the women in your group. They will learn from that involvement as well as from listening to the interesting and entertaining presentations. A complete outline for each of the fourteen (two extra!) programs, from clever roll call ideas to the closing prayer, will enable your group to have well-rounded, inspirational meetings.